D1278991

This book belongs to:

....

....

Edited by Lesley Sims
Research by Emma Helborough

First published in 2006 by Usborne Publishing Ltd., 83-85 Saffron Hill, London EC1N 8RT, England.
www.usborne.com. Printed in Dubai. UE. First published in America in 2006.

Usborne

Nursery Rhyme Treasury

Illustrated by
Dubravka Kolanovic

Designed by Hannah Ahmed
Compiled by Susanna Davidson

Contents

Animal Rhymes

Action Rhymes

Girls and Boys

Kings & Queens & Candlestick-Makers

Counting Rhymes

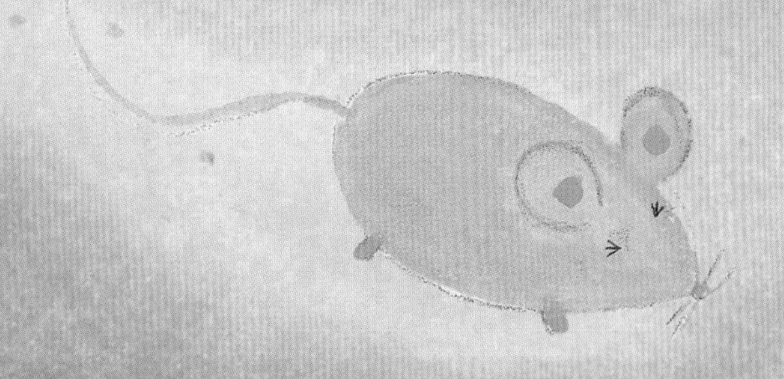

Rhymes for All Seasons

Bedtime Rhymes

Animal Rhymes

Old MacDonald

Old MacDonald had a farm,
Ee-i-ee-i-oh!
And on that farm he had some chicks,
Ee-i-ee-i-oh!
With a cluck-cluck here,
And a cluck-cluck there,
Here a cluck, there a cluck,
Everywhere a cluck-cluck
Old MacDonald had a farm,
Ee-i-ee-i-oh!

Old MacDonald had a farm,
Ee-i-ee-i-oh!
And on that farm he had some cows,
Ee-i-ee-i-oh!
With a moo-moo here,
And a moo-moo there,
Here a moo, there a moo,
Everywhere a moo-moo
Old MacDonald had a farm,
Ee-i-ee-i-oh!

Old MacDonald had a farm,
Ee-i-ee-i-oh!
And on that farm he had some pigs,
Ee-i-ee-i-oh!
With an oink-oink here,
And an oink-oink there,
Here an oink, there an oink,
Everywhere an oink-oink
Old MacDonald had a farm,
Ee-i-ee-i-oh!

Old MacDonald had a farm,
Ee-i-ee-i-oh!
And on that farm he had some sheep,
Ee-i-ee-i-oh!
With a baa-baa here,
And a baa-baa there,
Here a baa, there a baa,
Everywhere a baa-baa
Old MacDonald had a farm,
Ee-i-ee-i-oh!

Baa, Baa, Black Sheep

Baa, baa, black sheep,
Have you any wool?
Yes sir, yes sir,
Three bags full:
One for the master,
And one for the dame,
And one for the little boy
Who lives down the lane.

Mary Had a Little Lamb

Mary had a little lamb,
Its fleece was white as snow,
And everywhere that Mary went,
The lamb was sure to go.

Mr. Frog Jumped Out of the Pond

Mr. Frog jumped out of the pond one day
And found himself in the rain.
Said he, "I'll get wet and I might catch a cold."
So he jumped into the pond again.

Pussycat, Pussycat

Pussycat, pussycat, where have you been?
I've been to London to visit the Queen.
Pussycat, pussycat, what did you there?
I frightened a little mouse under her chair.

Three Little Kittens

Three little kittens they lost their mittens,
And they began to cry.
Oh, Mother dear, we sadly fear,
Our mittens we have lost.
What! Lost your mittens?
You naughty kittens!
Then you shall have no pie.
Mee-ow, mee-ow, mee-ow.

The three little kittens, they found their mittens,
And they began to cry.
Oh, Mother dear, see here, see here,
Our mittens we have found.
What! Found your mittens?
You darling kittens,
Then you shall have some pie.
Purr-r, purr-r, purr-r.

Little Miss Muffet

Little Miss Muffet,
Sat on a tuffet,
Eating her curds and whey;
Along came a spider,
Who sat down beside her,
And frightened Miss Muffet away.

Three Blind Mice

Three blind mice, three blind mice,
See how they run! See how they run!
They all ran after the farmer's wife
Who cut off their tails with a carving knife,
Did you ever see such a thing in your life
As three blind mice?

Hickory, Dickory, Dock

Hickory, dickory, dock!
The mouse ran up the clock;
The clock struck one,
The mouse ran down,
Hickory, dickory, dock!

Animal Fair

I went to the animal fair,
The birds and the beasts were there,
The big baboon by the light of the moon
Was combing his auburn hair.
The monkey fell out of his bunk,
And slid down the elephant's trunk,
The elephant sneezed and fell on his knees,
But what became of the monkey,
monkey,
monkey,
monkey. . . . . . .

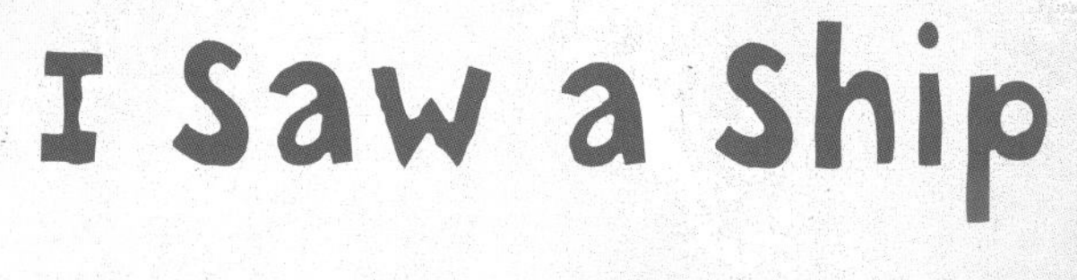

I saw a ship a-sailing,
A-sailing on the sea;
And, oh! it was all laden
With pretty things for thee!

There were comfits in the cabin,
And apples in the hold;
The sails were made of silk,
And the masts were made of gold.

The four and twenty sailors
That stood between the decks,
Were four and twenty white mice
With chains about their necks.

The captain was a duck,
With a packet on his back;
And when the ship began to move,
The captain said, "Quack! Quack!"

Action Rhymes

The Wheels on the Bus

The wheels on the bus go round and round,
Round and round, round and round.
The wheels on the bus go round and round,
All day long!

Roll one hand over the other

Keep rolling them on the word "round"

The people on the bus go chat, chat, chat,
Chat, chat, chat; chat, chat, chat.
The people on the bus go chat, chat, chat,
All day long!

Snap together your fingers and thumb

Repeat this action on the word "chat"

The bell on the bus goes ding, ding, ding,
Ding, ding, ding; ding, ding, ding.
The bell on the bus goes ding, ding, ding,
All day long!

The driver on the bus goes beep, beep, beep,
Beep, beep, beep; beep, beep, beep.
The driver on the bus goes beep, beep, beep,
All day long!

Heads, Shoulders, Knees and Toes

Heads,

shoulders,

Touch your head

Touch your shoulders

knees

and toes,

Touch your knees

Touch your toes

knees and toes.

Touch your knees and toes again!

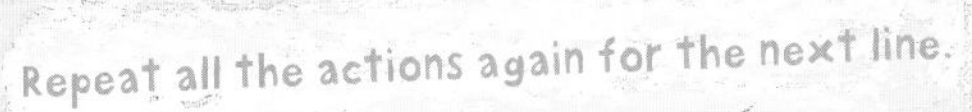

Heads, shoulders, knees and toes,
knees and toes.

And eyes

Touch your eyes

and ears

Touch your ears

and mouth

Touch your mouth

and nose,

Touch your nose

Heads, shoulders, knees and toes,
knees and toes.

Repeat the first actions
again for the last line.

Do Your Ears Hang Low?

Do your ears hang low?

Do they wobble to and fro?

Can you tie them in a knot?

Can you tie them in a bow?

Can you throw them o'er your shoulder,

Like a continental soldier?

Do your ears hang low?

Repeat the first actions again for the last line.

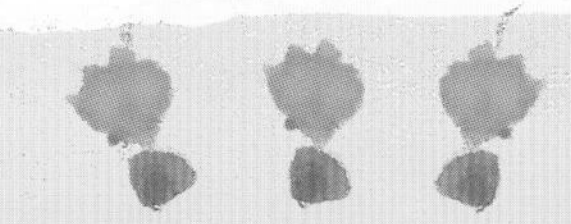

This Little Piggy

This little piggy went to market,
This little piggy stayed at home,
This little piggy had roast beef,
This little piggy had none,
This little piggy said,
"Wee, wee, wee," all the way home.

Wiggle your child's toes with each line. Start with the big toe and end with the little toe.

On the last line, tickle your child wherever they're most ticklish.

Round and Round the Garden

Round and round the garden

Like a teddy bear;

One step, two step,

Tickle you under there!

As you say the first two lines, trace your finger around your child's palm

tickle

tickle

tickle

tickle

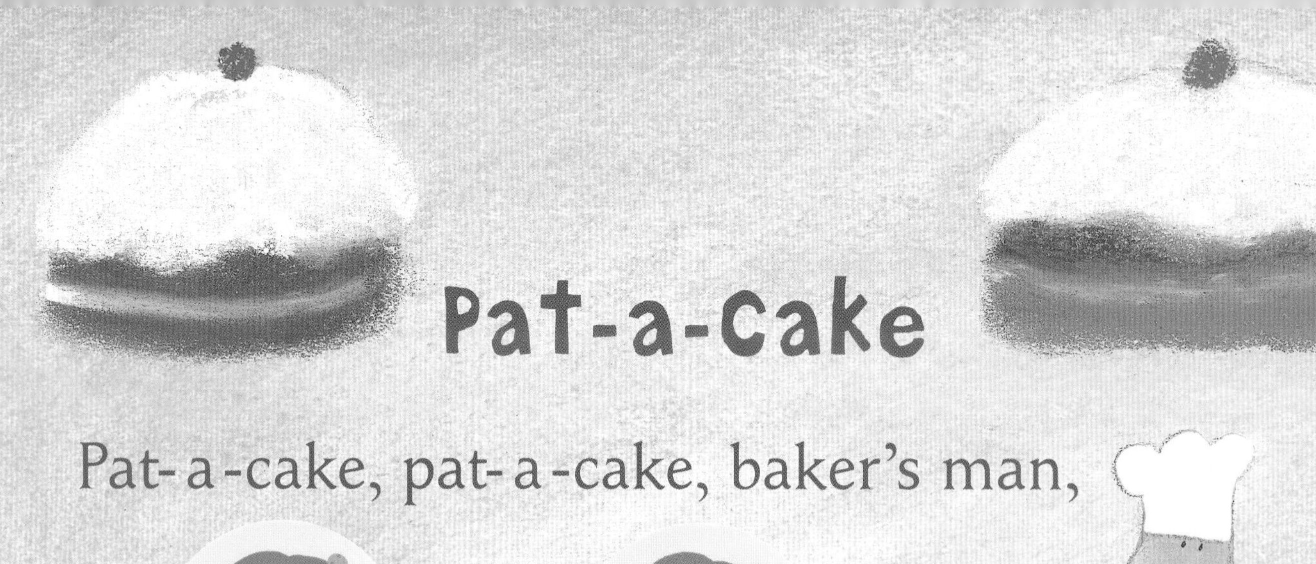

Pat-a-Cake

Pat-a-cake, pat-a-cake, baker's man,

Bake me a cake as fast as you can.

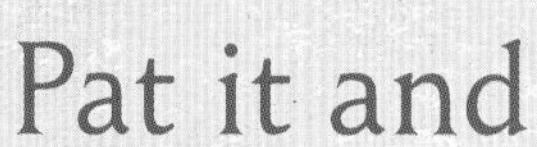

Pat it and

prick it and mark it with B

And put it in the oven for Baby and me.

If You're Happy and You Know It

If you're happy and you know it, clap your hands.
If you're happy and you know it, clap your hands.
If you're happy and you know it
and you really want to show it,
If you're happy and you know it, clap your hands.

Clap your hands twice after the first, second and fifth lines.

If you're happy and you know it, stomp your feet.
If you're happy and you know it, stomp your feet.
If you're happy and you know it
and you really want to show it,
If you're happy and you know it, stomp your feet.

Stomp your feet twice after the first, second and fifth lines.

If you're happy and you know it, shout "Hooray!"
If you're happy and you know it, shout "Hooray!"
If you're happy and you know it
and you really want to show it,
If you're happy and you know it, shout "Hooray!"

Shout "Hooray" once after the first, second and fifth lines.

Girls and Boys

Monday's Child

Monday's child is fair of face,
Tuesday's child is full of grace,
Wednesday's child is full of woe,
Thursday's child has far to go,
Friday's child is loving and giving,
Saturday's child works hard for a living,
But the child that is born on the Sabbath Day,
Is bonny and blithe and good and gay.

What Are Little Boys Made Of?

What are little boys made of?
"Frogs and snails, and puppy dogs' tails
That's what little boys are made of!"
What are little girls made of?
"Sugar and spice and all things nice
That's what little girls are made of!"

There Was a Little Girl

There was a little girl who had a little curl
Right in the middle of her forehead.
When she was good, she was very, very good
But when she was bad, she was horrid.

Little Bo-Peep

Little Bo-Peep has lost her sheep,
And doesn't know where to find them;
Leave them alone, and they'll come home,
Wagging their tails behind them.

Jack and Jill

Jack and Jill went up the hill
To fetch a pail of water;
Jack fell down and broke his crown,
And Jill came tumbling after.

Up Jack got, and home did trot,
As fast as he could caper;
He went to bed to mend his head
With vinegar and brown paper.

Little Jack Horner

Little Jack Horner
Sat in a corner,
Eating a mincemeat pie;
He stuck in his thumb,
And pulled out a plum,
And said, "What a good boy am I!"

Seesaw, Margery Daw

Seesaw, Margery Daw,
Johnny shall have a new master;
He shall have but a penny a day,
Because he can't work any faster.

Pop Goes the Weasel

Half a pound of tuppenny rice,
Half a pound of treacle,
That's the way the money goes,
Pop goes the weasel!

All around the carpenter's bench,
The monkey chased the weasel,
That's the way the money goes,
Pop goes the weasel!

Georgy Porgy

Georgy Porgy, pudding and pie,
Kissed the girls and made them cry.
When the boys came out to play,
Georgy Porgy ran away.

Curly Locks

Curly Locks, Curly Locks, wilt thou be mine?
Thou shalt not wash dishes, nor yet feed the swine,
But sit on a cushion and sew a fine seam,
And feed upon strawberries, sugar and cream!

Lucy Locket

Lucy Locket lost her pocket,
Kitty Fisher found it;
Not a penny was there in it,
Only ribbon round it.

Polly Put the Kettle On

Polly put the kettle on,
Polly put the kettle on,
Polly put the kettle on,
We'll all have tea.

Sukey take it off again,
Sukey take it off again,
Sukey take it off again,
They've all gone away.

Hot Cross Buns

Hot cross buns!
Hot cross buns!
One a penny,
Two a penny,
Hot cross buns!

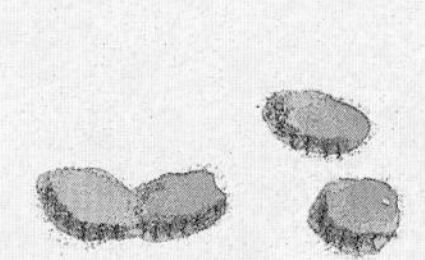

If you have no daughters,
Give them to your sons;
One a penny,
Two a penny,
Hot cross buns!

Simple Simon

Simple Simon met a pieman
Going to the fair;
Said Simple Simon to the pieman,
"Let me taste your ware."

Said the pieman unto Simon,
"Show me first your penny."
Said Simple Simon to the pieman,
"Sir, I haven't any."

Kings & Queens & Candlestick-makers

Humpty Dumpty

Humpty Dumpty sat on a wall,
Humpty Dumpty had a great fall;
All the king's horses and all the king's men
Couldn't put Humpty together again.

I'm the King of the Castle

I'm the king of the castle!
You're a dirty rascal!

The Grand Old Duke of York

Oh the grand old Duke of York
He had ten thousand men
He marched them up to the top of the hill
And he marched them down again.
And when they were up, they were up,
And when they were down, they were down.
And when they were only halfway up,
They were neither up nor down.

Old King Cole

Old King Cole was a merry old soul,
And a merry old soul was he;
He called for his pipe in the middle of the night
And he called for his fiddlers three.

Every fiddler had a fine fiddle,
And a very fine fiddle had he.
Oh there's none so rare as can compare
With King Cole and his fiddlers three!

Sing a Song of Sixpence

Sing a song of sixpence, a pocket full of rye,
Four and twenty blackbirds baked in a pie.
When the pie was opened, the birds began to sing,
Wasn't that a dainty dish to set before the King?

The King was in his counting-house, counting out his money;
The Queen was in the dining room, eating bread and honey;
The maid was in the garden, hanging out the clothes,
When down came a blackbird and pecked off her nose.

I Had a Little Nut Tree

I had a little nut tree,
Nothing would it bear,
But a silver nutmeg
And a golden pear.
The King of Spain's daughter
Came to visit me,
And all for the sake of my little nut tree.

Old Mother Hubbard

Old Mother Hubbard went to the cupboard,
To fetch her poor dog a bone.
But when she got there, the cupboard was bare,
And so the poor dog had none.

Jack Sprat

Jack Sprat could eat no fat,
His wife could eat no lean,
And so between them both, you see,
They licked the platter clean.

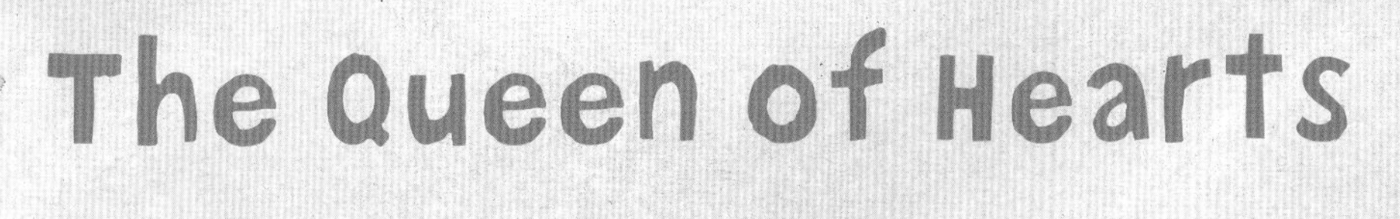

The Queen of Hearts

The Queen of Hearts,
She made some tarts,
All on a summer's day;
The Knave of Hearts,
He stole those tarts,
And took them clean away.

The King of Hearts
Called for the tarts,
And beat the Knave full sore;
The Knave of Hearts
Brought back the tarts,
And vowed he'd steal no more.

Row, Row, Row Your Boat

Row, row, row your boat,
Gently down the stream.
Merrily, merrily, merrily, merrily,
Life is but a dream.

Rub-a-Dub-Dub

Rub-a-dub-dub,
Three men in a tub,
And who do you think they be?
The butcher, the baker,
The candlestick-maker,
Turn 'em out, knaves all three!

Counting Rhymes

The Animals Went in Two by Two

The animals went in two by two,
Hurrah! Hurrah!
The animals went in two by two,
Hurrah! Hurrah!
The animals went in two by two,
The elephant and the kangaroo
And they all went into the ark,
Just to get out of the rain.

The animals went in three by three,
Hurrah! Hurrah!
The animals went in three by three,
Hurrah! Hurrah!
The animals went in three by three,
The wasp, the ant and the bumblebee
And they all went into the ark,
Just to get out of the rain.

The animals went in four by four,
Hurrah! Hurrah!
The animals went in four by four,
Hurrah! Hurrah!
The animals went in four by four,
The great hippopotamus got stuck in the door
And they all went into the ark,
Just to get out of the rain.

One, Two, Three, Four, Five

One, two, three, four, five,
Once I caught a fish alive;
Six, seven, eight, nine, ten,
Then I let it go again.

Why did you let it go?
Because it bit my finger so.
Which finger did it bite?
This little finger on the right.

One Potato, Two Potato

One potato, two potato,
Three potato, four,
Five potato, six potato,
Seven potato, more!

Five Fat Sausages

Five fat sausages sizzling in a pan,
One went pop and another went BANG!

Four fat sausages sizzling in a pan,
One went pop and another went BANG!

Three fat sausages sizzling in a pan,
One went pop and another went
BANG!

Two fat sausages sizzling in a pan,
One went pop and another went
BANG!

One fat sausage sizzling in a pan,
All of a sudden it went BANG!

No more sausages sizzling in a pan!

Five Little Ducks

Five little ducks went swimming one day
Over the hill and far away.
Mother duck said, "Quack, quack, quack, quack."
But only four little ducks came swimming back.

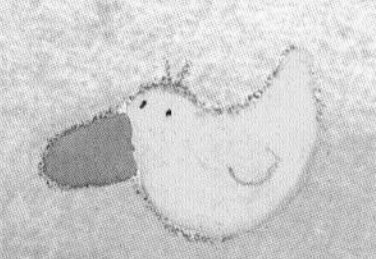

Four little ducks went swimming one day
Over the hill and far away.
Mother duck said, "Quack, quack, quack, quack."
But only three little ducks came swimming back.

Three little ducks went swimming one day
Over the hill and far away.
Mother duck said, "Quack, quack, quack, quack."
But only two little ducks came swimming back.

Two little ducks went swimming one day
Over the hill and far away.
Mother duck said, "Quack, quack, quack, quack."
But only one little duck came swimming back.

One little duck went swimming one day
Over the hill and far away.
Mother duck said, "Quack, quack, quack, quack."
And all five little ducks came swimming back.

Five Little Monkeys

Five little monkeys jumping on the bed,
One fell off and bumped his head.
Mama called the doctor and the doctor said,
"No more monkeys jumping on the bed!"

Four little monkeys jumping on the bed,
One fell off and bumped his head.
Mama called the doctor and the doctor said,
"No more monkeys jumping on the bed!"

Three little monkeys jumping on the bed,
One fell off and bumped his head.
Mama called the doctor and the doctor said,
"No more monkeys jumping on the bed!"

Two little monkeys jumping on the bed,
One fell off and bumped his head.
Mama called the doctor and the doctor said,
"No more monkeys jumping on the bed!"

One little monkey jumping on the bed,
One fell off and bumped his head.
Mama called the doctor and the doctor said,
"Put those monkeys back in bed!"

Five Little Speckled Frogs

Five little speckled frogs,
Sat on a speckled log,
Eating the most delicious bugs
Yum-yum!
One jumped into the pool,
Where it was nice and cool,
Then there were four green speckled frogs
Glub! Glub!

Four little speckled frogs,
Sat on a speckled log,
Eating the most delicious bugs
Yum-yum!
One jumped into the pool,
Where it was nice and cool,
Then there were three green speckled frogs
Glub! Glub!

Three little speckled frogs,
Sat on a speckled log,
Eating the most delicious bugs
Yum-yum!
One jumped into the pool,
Where it was nice and cool,
Then there were two green speckled frogs
Glub! Glub!

Two little speckled frogs,
Sat on a speckled log,
Eating the most delicious bugs
Yum-yum!
One jumped into the pool,
Where it was nice and cool,
Then there was one green speckled frog
Glub! Glub!

Ten in a Bed

There were ten in a bed and the little one said,
"Roll over, roll over!"
So they all rolled over and one fell out.

There were nine in a bed and the little one said,
"Roll over, roll over!"
So they all rolled over and one fell out.

There were eight in a bed and the little one said,
"Roll over, roll over!"
So they all rolled over and one fell out.

There were seven in a bed and the little one said,
"Roll over, roll over!"
So they all rolled over and one fell out.

There were six in a bed and the little one said,
"Roll over, roll over!"
So they all rolled over and one fell out.

There were five in a bed and the little one said,
"Roll over, roll over!"
So they all rolled over and one fell out.

There were four in a bed and the little one said,
"Roll over, roll over!"
So they all rolled over and one fell out.

There were three in a bed and the little one said,
"Roll over, roll over!"
So they all rolled over and one fell out.

There were two in a bed and the little one said,
"Roll over, roll over!"
So they all rolled over and one fell out.

There was one in a bed and the little one said,
"Goodnight!"

Rhymes for all Seasons

Mary, Mary, Quite Contrary

Mary, Mary, quite contrary,
How does your garden grow?
With silver bells and cockle shells,
And pretty maids all in a row.

Little Boy Blue

Little Boy Blue, come blow your horn,
The sheep's in the meadow, the cow's in the corn;
But where is the little boy who looks after the sheep?
He's under the haystack, fast asleep!

Lavender's Blue

Lavender's blue, dilly dilly,
Lavender's green,
When I am King, dilly dilly,
You shall be Queen.

Who told you so, dilly dilly,
Who told you so?
'Twas my own heart, dilly dilly,
That told me so.

Call up your friends, dilly dilly,
Set them to work,
Some to the cart, dilly dilly,
Some to the fork.

Some to the hay, dilly dilly,
Some to thresh corn,
Whilst you and I, dilly dilly,
Keep ourselves warm.

Lavender's blue, dilly dilly,
Lavender's green,
When I am King, dilly dilly,
You shall be Queen.

Lavender's green, dilly dilly,
Lavender's blue,
If you love me, dilly dilly,
I will love you.

It's Raining, It's Pouring

It's raining, it's pouring,
The old man is snoring;
He went to bed,
And bumped his head
And couldn't get up in the morning.

Rain, Rain, Go Away

Rain, rain, go away,
Come again another day.

Doctor Foster

Doctor Foster
Went to Gloucester
In a shower of rain.
He stepped in a puddle
Right up to his middle
And never went there again!

The North Wind Doth Blow

The north wind doth blow and we shall have snow,
And what will poor robin do then, poor thing?
He'll sit in a barn and keep himself warm
And hide his head under his wing, poor thing.

Bedtime Rhymes

She'll Be Coming Round the Mountain

She'll be coming round the mountain when she comes,
She'll be coming round the mountain when she comes,
She'll be coming round the mountain,
Coming round the mountain,
Coming round the mountain when she comes.

She'll be driving six white horses when she comes,
She'll be driving six white horses when she comes,
She'll be driving six white horses,
Driving six white horses,
Driving six white horses when
she comes.

She'll be wearing pink pyjamas when she comes,
She'll be wearing pink pyjamas when she comes,
She'll be wearing pink pyjamas,
Wearing pink pyjamas,
Wearing pink pyjamas when she comes.

Oh we'll all go out to meet her when she comes,
Oh we'll all go out to meet her when she comes,
Oh we'll all go out to meet her,
All go out to meet her,
All go out to meet her when she comes.

Girls and Boys Come Out to Play

Girls and boys, come out to play,
The moon doth shine as bright as day;
Leave your supper, and leave your sleep,
And come with your playfellows into the street.

Come with a whoop, come with a call,
Come with a good will or not at all;
Up the ladder and down the wall,
A half-penny roll will serve us all.

Wee Willie Winkie

Wee Willie Winkie runs through the town,
Upstairs and downstairs in his nightgown,
Tapping at the window and crying through the lock,
"Are all the children in their beds? It's past eight o'clock!"

I See the Moon

I see the moon, the moon sees me
Under the shade of the old oak tree.
Please let the light that shines on me
Shine on the one I love.
Over the mountains, over the sea,
That's where my heart is longing to be.
Please let the light that shines on me
Shine on the one I love.

There Was an Old Woman

There was an old woman tossed up in a basket,
Seventeen times as high as the moon.
Where she was going I couldn't but ask it,
For in her hand she carried a broom.
"Old woman, old woman, old woman," said I,
"Where are you going to up so high?"
"To brush the cobwebs off the sky!"
"May I go with you?"
"Aye, by-and-by."

Twinkle, Twinkle, Little Star

Twinkle, twinkle, little star,
How I wonder what you are,
Up above the world so high,
Like a diamond in the sky;
Twinkle, twinkle, little star,
How I wonder what you are.

Rock-a-Bye Baby

Rock-a-bye baby, on the tree top,
When the wind blows, the cradle will rock.
When the bough breaks, the cradle will fall,
And down will come baby, cradle and all.

Hey Diddle Diddle

Hey diddle diddle,
The cat and the fiddle,
The cow jumped over the moon;
The little dog laughed
To see such fun,
And the dish ran away with the spoon.

Sleep, Baby, Sleep

Sleep, baby, sleep,
Your father tends the sheep,
Your mother shakes the dreamland tree,
And from it fall sweet dreams for thee,
Sleep, baby, sleep,
Sleep, baby, sleep.

Sleep, baby, sleep,
Our cottage vale is deep,
The little lamb is on the green,
With snowy fleece so soft and clean,
Sleep, baby, sleep,
Sleep, baby, sleep.

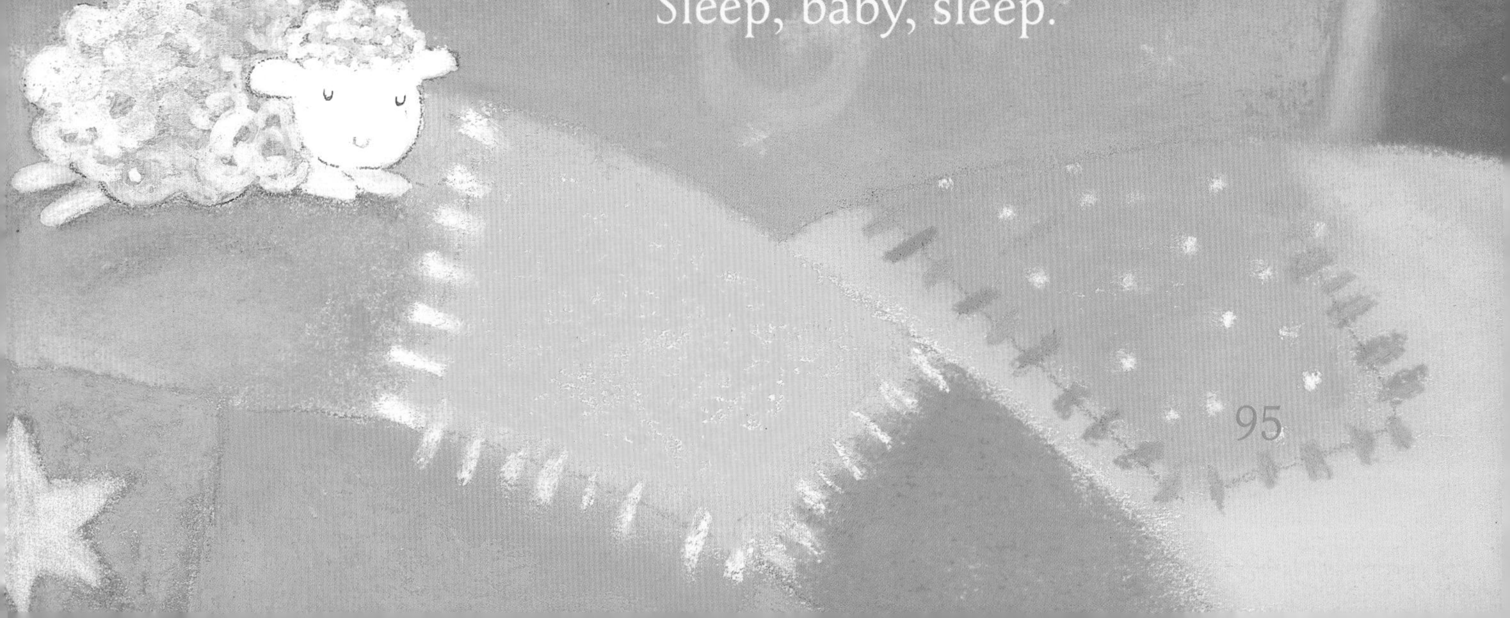

Index of Nursery Rhymes